What does it mean to be a
Wheelchair User

Louise Spilsbury

Heinemann
LIBRARY

www.heinemann.co.uk/library
Visit our website to find out more information about Heinemann Library books.

To order:
 Phone 44 (0) 1865 888066
 Send a fax to 44 (0) 1865 314091
 Visit the Heinemann Bookshop at www.heinemann.co.uk/library to browse our
catalogue and order online.

First published in Great Britain by Heinemann Library,
Halley Court, Jordan Hill, Oxford OX2 8EJ,
a division of Reed Educational and Professional Publishing Ltd.
Heinemann is a registered trademark of Reed Educational and Professional Publishing Ltd.

OXFORD MELBOURNE AUCKLAND
JOHANNESBURG BLANTYRE GABORONE
IBADAN PORTSMOUTH (NH) USA CHICAGO

Designed by AMR
Originated by Dot Gradations
Printed by Wing King Tong, Hong Kong.

ISBN 0 431 13939 3
07 06 05 04 03 02
10 9 8 7 6 5 4 3 2 1

British Library Cataloguing in Publication Data
Spilsbury, Louise
  What does it mean to be a wheelchair user?
  1.Wheelchairs – Juvenle literature 2.Physically
  handicapped – Juvenile literature
  I.Title II.Wheelchair user
  305.9'0816

Acknowledgements
The publishers would like to thank the following for permission to reproduce photographs: Association of
Wheelchair Children: pp.8, 9, 14, 16, 17, 22; Bubbles/Amanda Knapp: p.26; Corbis: p.27; Corbis/Tom
Nebbia: p.7; Corbis/Michael Pole: pp.5, 6; Sally and Richard Greenhill: pp.4, 24, 25; Popperphoto: p.15;
Chris Schwartz: pp.11, 12, 13, 18, 19, 20, 21, 28, 29; Science Photo Library: p.10; John Walmsley: p.22.

Special thanks to: Daniel, Fay and Lee.

The publishers would also like to thank: the Treloar Trust, the Association of Wheelchair Children and
Julie Johnson, PHSE Consultant Trainer and Writer, for their help in the preparation of this book.

Cover photograph reproduced with permission of the Association of Wheelchair Children.

Every effort has been made to contact copyright holders of any material reproduced in this book.
Any omissions will be rectified in subsequent printings if notice is given to the publishers.

Contents

Any words appearing in the text in bold, **like this**,
are explained in the Glossary.

Using a wheelchair

Do you know someone who uses a wheelchair? Perhaps you use one yourself? Wheelchairs are what their name suggests – chairs with four wheels that can move in all directions. People use wheelchairs if they find walking difficult or if they cannot walk. A wheelchair is a piece of equipment to help you get around, just as glasses help people to see and braces help teeth to grow straight.

There are many different reasons why people cannot walk very well. Some people cannot use their legs from the time they are born. Others have been injured in a car accident. Some people have fallen off a horse or out of a tree and damaged their legs, back or **brain**. Others have had an illness that caused the problem. Many children who use wheelchairs can walk quite well indoors, but need to use a wheelchair outdoors.

With a wheelchair to help, people who cannot walk easily can get around on their own to do everyday things, such as going to the park.

Sitting in a wheelchair does not change who you are. A wheelchair is simply a tool to help you get around.

People use wheelchairs in different ways. Some people who use wheelchairs have to use them for only a short time, perhaps because they broke their legs in an accident. Other people need to use a wheelchair for most of the time, or for their whole lives. Some of these people spend most of the day in their wheelchair; they learn how to use a wheelchair to get around easily at home and at school, and when they are out and about. Others use a wheelchair for only some of the time, for example, when they have to go a long way from home.

People who use wheelchairs are the same as everyone else – but they have a different way of getting around. They have the same feelings, the same needs and the same desires as the next person. They go to school, do their homework, go shopping, listen to music and hang out with their friends, just like anyone else.

Who uses wheelchairs?

People use wheelchairs for many different reasons. Some people cannot walk because they have or have had an illness that means they cannot move easily. Others may have lost or damaged one or both legs in an accident. It may be because their **spinal cord** is damaged, or because the part of the **brain** that controls leg movement does not work properly.

When someone cannot walk

The brain is the body's control centre. It sends signals along the spinal cord to **nerves** in other parts of your body, telling them what to do and when to do it. If someone cannot walk, it usually means that parts of their legs are not getting the signals from the brain, or are not responding to them. This may be because their legs are damaged in some way. It may be because the part of the brain that controls the legs is damaged. Or the spinal cord, which takes messages between the brain and the legs, may be damaged.

Simon uses a wheelchair because his spinal cord was damaged in a car accident. He is healthy – he just needs to use a wheelchair to get around.

Some young people use wheelchairs because they have an illness or a **condition** that affects their ability to walk. They may have been born with it, developed it during or after birth, or when they were older. Some have to use a wheelchair all the time. Some may be able to walk a little but are unsteady on their feet, or get tired quickly. For others, it is painful to walk.

Diseases and conditions that cause walking difficulties include **muscular dystrophy**, **spina bifida** and **cerebral palsy**. You may have heard these names before. Muscular dystrophy is a disease that makes the muscles get weaker, and some people with it have trouble walking. Spina bifida affects a person's spinal cord. Many children with spina bifida do not use wheelchairs at all. Others may have **paralysis** in some parts of the body so that they cannot walk. People who have cerebral palsy may have difficulty walking because their limbs feel stiff or difficult to control. The reason for this is that the part of their brain that controls movement has been damaged.

Jason uses a wheelchair because he has cerebral palsy. He does not need the wheelchair all the time. Sometimes he walks with the help of crutches.

Kinds of wheelchairs

Wheelchairs come in a huge range of colours, styles and sizes to suit individual needs and tastes. Some people buy their own wheelchairs. Others have them on permanent loan from their hospital or local **wheelchair service**. There are three main types of wheelchairs: attendant-propelled, self-propelled and electric.

Attendant-propelled wheelchairs are designed to be propelled (pushed) by a person walking behind. Young people are often pushed by their parents, or by a helper if they are at school. It is less easy to be independent when you have to rely on someone else to move you around.

Some people choose colourful new wheelchairs and even add their own stickers to personalize them.

People in self-propelled wheelchairs push themselves. They turn the wheel rim on the outside of each of the wheels on their chair to make it move. However, not everyone can do this. It takes quite a bit of strength and flexibility in your shoulders, arms and hands to control a self-propelled wheelchair.

Electric wheelchairs

Electric (or power) wheelchairs run on batteries. They are usually more expensive than the other kinds of wheelchair, but many people find them very useful. These wheelchairs have electric controllers so the user can drive smoothly, brake easily and make the wheelchair move in the direction they want to go at the touch of a hand. Some have controllers on the arm of the wheelchair. Some of these look a bit like a joystick you might use for a computer game. Some people use electric wheelchairs because they are unable to propel themselves; others simply find them easier to use than self-propelled wheelchairs.

Some wheelchairs are especially adapted for different sports. This wheelchair is especially lightweight, strong and stable for road racing.

Children who use electric wheelchairs always have a spare chair. The electric wheelchair is usually plugged in to charge up overnight. They use a manual wheelchair or a walking frame to get about in the evening or if they need to get up at night.

People who help

Everyone who uses a wheelchair has different needs and these may change at different times of their lives. The kind of help they need also depends on whether the person has any other difficulties besides not being able to walk. If someone has **cerebral palsy** they may need support at school with learning, or support from a **speech and language therapist** to help them speak clearly. Almost everyone who uses a wheelchair will have help from **physiotherapists** and **occupational therapists** at some point in their lives.

Physiotherapists

Physiotherapists are trained to help people with their physical movements. They work with people to find out how well they can move and they decide when someone needs to have a wheelchair. They help people choose the wheelchair that is right for them.

They may also plan exercises for people. These exercises can help to reduce any discomfort people have from sitting in a wheelchair a lot. People should also do the exercises at home. If they do them regularly, they can help keep their body strong and healthy.

Physiotherapists help people improve their physical abilities.

Occupational therapists

Occupational therapists help people who have physical difficulties to live as independently as possible. They give advice on how to cope with everyday physical tasks such as washing, dressing or putting on socks and shoes. They also help wheelchair users find solutions to practical problems they have. For example, an occupational therapist might help a wheelchair user come up with a plan to get across school in time for lunch. They help the person to practise the activity in stages, until they are happy that they can manage it themselves.

Everyone learns to do things in their own time. Some people need to see an occupational therapist for only a short time; others may need their help for longer. Some people find that they don't need help for a while but when something in their life changes, perhaps when they change schools, they go back to the therapist to help them work out ways of coping with a new space.

Meet Daniel

My name is Daniel and I'm fourteen years old. I've got a brother called Kieran who is eleven and a sister, Nicola, who is thirteen. We get on well together. As well as my mum and dad, we've also got three cats. Sometimes they bring mice into the house and mum has to chase them out. The cats like lying on my lap.

When I'm at home I use a manual wheelchair because my electric one is too big for inside the house, and my family push me around in it. My dad is having a new bedroom built for me. It will be a big one on the side of the house that will be easier for me to get around in.

I really like playing and watching football. We've got satellite television so I can watch all the matches. I play football with my dad and my brother. We've got a big garden to play in. We don't have goals or anything; we just muck around. The other thing I really like doing is going to discos. I really like discos.

The other sport I like is boxing and I watch that on telly, too. Sometimes I stay up late watching TV and then I like to lie in the next morning. I'd say bed is my favourite place, and I really like sleeping and snoring!

I stay at my school in the week and come home at weekends. I can use my electric wheelchair at school. I can go really fast in it. When I go out with my brother and sister I go zooming about ahead of them. I went on a course to learn how to use it when I first got my electric wheelchair. Pavements are really tricky. When I'm at home, my mum usually helps me up and down pavements.

At school, my favourite thing is going on the Internet. We can use the computers in class to look at the Internet after lessons and during break times. That is what I like doing best at playtime. My old school was really small. I like my new school much better. There are loads of people in my class but everyone in my class is my friend. We all get on really well.

Coping with a wheelchair

Each person who uses a wheelchair is an individual and has different ways of coping. How well they get on with it may depend on the reasons why they use a wheelchair, or how long they have been using one.

Someone who has been using a wheelchair since they were very young may be very confident about getting around. They have had lots of time to learn how to use a wheelchair and to find ways of dealing with tricky situations. People who have only just begun to use a wheelchair, or who have only been using one for a short while, may find it hard to adjust at first. They may get tired, because it takes a lot of hard work and determination to learn to use a wheelchair properly.

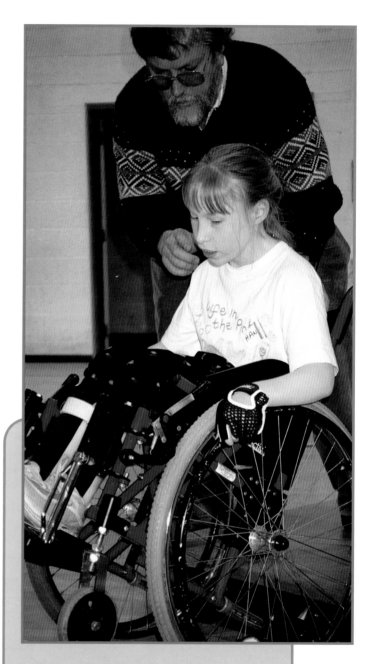

It can take a lot of hard work and effort to learn to use a wheelchair.

How does it feel?

You know how it is. Sometimes you feel happy, confident and ready for anything. At other times, life seems to be full of obstacles. Individual wheelchair users feel differently at different times as well. They have days when they worry about friends, schoolwork or money, just like anyone else. Sometimes they may feel down because using a wheelchair can make them feel different, or can make them stand out in a way they don't want to. They may feel frustrated if someone wrongly assumes that not being able to walk means they are unable to do lots of other things as well. It can be good to talk to family and friends at times like these.

Most of the time, wheelchair users, like anyone else, just get on with their lives. Many even say that being a wheelchair user has made them even more determined to make the most of their life and the things they can do.

Tanni Grey-Thompson did not think that because she was a wheelchair user she could not play sport. She has **spina bifida** and has been using a wheelchair since she was eight. Now she is a world-famous wheelchair-racing star who has won gold medals at the **Paralympics**.

Learning to use a wheelchair

When you see someone going past in a wheelchair, it might look like a straightforward thing to do. It might even look like an easy option if you have just been walking a long way and your legs are tired! Think again. All wheelchair users, whether they use manual (hand-propelled) or electric wheelchairs, have to work hard to get to grips with their machines and the obstacles they meet when they are out on the street.

Learning to use a wheelchair is a bit like learning to use any vehicle. You don't just have to master the chair itself. You also have to learn how to deal with kerbs, uneven pavements, slopes, very bumpy ground, tight corners and all kinds of obstacles, from badly parked cars to bustling crowds of people. Wheelchair users need to learn all these things so that they can be independent and do things like go out to the cinema or a friend's house without having to ask other people for help.

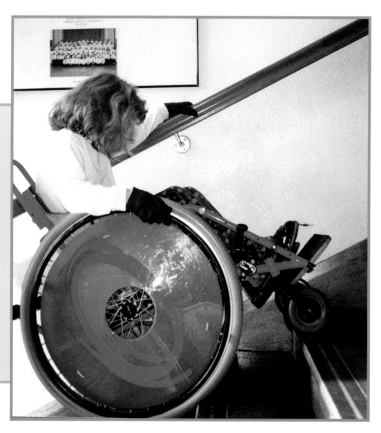

Most children are confident about using a wheelchair indoors, and they don't have much trouble learning to turn left and right, and to move forwards and stop. They do need special training to learn how to go down a flight of stairs safely.

On the road!

As a wheelchair user, the most important things to learn are the rules of the road – rules such as where it is safe to cross and how to be seen clearly by road users. If you have spent some of your time being pushed by parents or helpers, you may never have learned these things. We all need to know what road signs mean, and when and where to cross roads safely.

It takes practice to be able to get up and down kerbs easily in a wheelchair, but it is well worth the effort as it makes you so much more independent.

Lots of wheelchair users have training to deal with the other main problem – kerbs. If you go straight off a kerb in a wheelchair, or hit it at an angle, you could be flung out of the chair and into the street. The key to being able to manage kerbs is knowing how to balance on your back wheels while moving. If you tip your chair backwards as you come off the kerb, you should be able to roll off the edge on your back wheels and land cleanly in the road. Getting up kerbs uses the same balancing skills, but takes even more practice.

Getting around

Knowing how to use your wheelchair is one thing, but what about using it to get around buildings, and on and off public transport? Today, many countries have laws to ensure that all new public buildings, such as shops, museums, libraries, sports centres and schools, are built so that people in wheelchairs can use them easily. Of course, many of the buildings we use every day were built in the past, so they were not designed with wheelchair users in mind. Think about some of the places you visit. Which of them would be difficult to get around in a wheelchair?

An international symbol

If you are a wheelchair user, it can be really frustrating to arrive at somewhere you want to visit only to find steps and narrow doorways making it impossible to get in. Look out for the wheelchair **access** symbol. It tells you what lifts and facilities, such as toilets, are specially designed for people who use wheelchairs. This is an international symbol. It means the same thing wherever in the world you see it.

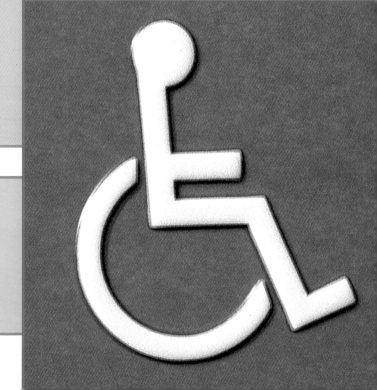

If you are a wheelchair user, this symbol shows you where facilities have been designed with you in mind.

Plan ahead: transport tricks!

If you are a wheelchair user, some forms of public transport are very difficult to use. If you go to a school a little way from home, the chances are that you are taken by your parents in the family car, or collected and dropped off by taxi. Some towns and cities have **mobility** buses which have ramps or platforms which can be lowered to allow a wheelchair user to get on or off, but these are not available everywhere.

If you are planning a day out or a holiday, the trick is to plan ahead. Phone taxi companies in advance to ask if they have vehicles with wheelchair access. If you are travelling by train, check if the train you want to travel on has somewhere you can sit in your wheelchair. Most stations should have ramps you can use to board the train and most trains have spaces for wheelchairs. It is also a good idea to get to stations and airports in plenty of time so that staff have time to sort out help for you.

With a bit of forward planning and determination, wheelchair users can go just about anywhere they want to go!

19

Meet Fay

Hi. I'm Fay. I use a wheelchair because I have **cerebral palsy**. I've been using a wheelchair since I was nearly six years old. I'm eleven years old now. At the moment I've got a sports wheelchair. I went on a wheelchair course to learn how to drive it. At first, I got sores on my hands because I wasn't used to it. Now I've got special gloves with leather padding to stop my hands rubbing. I can go fast in my chair because it's so light. I go to discos in my wheelchair and dance with my friend Liam. He's got an electric wheelchair. I'm getting one soon, but I'm only going to use it after school when my hands get tired. The electric one has got a huge battery that fits in the back to make it go. You need to charge it up overnight so it's ready the next day.

It's pretty easy to get about in a wheelchair most of the time. When I go to the cinema there's a big space where they have taken a seat out for you. You can sit in it in your wheelchair and there are two or three seats next to it where your friends or family can sit.

At home, I have a lift that goes through the ceiling so I can get upstairs to my bedroom. In my bedroom I've got a nice wide computer table so I can get my wheelchair under it properly. The keyboard controls are on a smaller section that slides out so it's right over my lap where I need it. One of my favourite hobbies is going on the Internet and looking at my favourite websites. I also do some of my schoolwork on the computer.

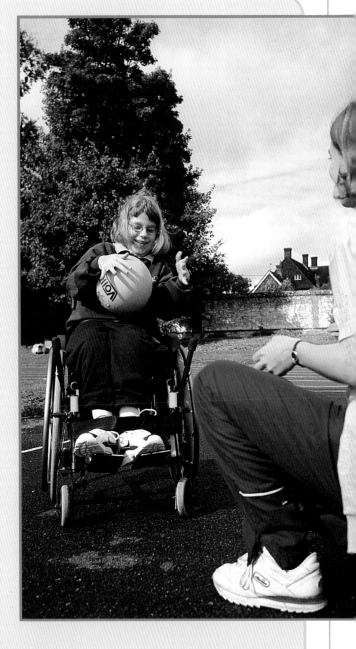

My school is fantastic. I stay there in the week and come home at weekends. We have discos and go swimming, and I also play football. I won a trophy for being the best girl goalie. When I go in goal, I get out of the chair and lie down on a mat with the net behind me. I lie in the middle of the goal and reach out to catch the ball. There is a special sort of guard to stop people in wheelchairs who are trying to score a goal from running into me. Being in a wheelchair is not as bad as some people think. Think of it from the wheelchair person's point of view – I'm very happy.

Life as a wheelchair user

We are all good at different things. We all have things we know we can do well, and others that we know we cannot do so well. Perhaps you have a friend who is great at football, while you never seem to get anywhere near the ball in a match, no matter how hard you try. Have you ever been picked on because of something you cannot do? It is annoying to be judged by what you cannot do, rather than the things you can do, isn't it?

This is how many people who use a wheelchair say they feel. They do most of the things other people do, and they don't want to be judged by the few things they cannot do. Most say they do not like the word 'disability'. They would rather concentrate on their abilities – the things they are good at. Having a positive attitude is good for all of us – it is good to think of the things you can do, or to find new, alternative ways of doing the things you want to do.

This wheelchair user is just the same as anyone else – with needs and feelings, and strengths and weaknesses like any other person.

How can you make a difference?

Wheelchair users don't want special treatment, but there are a few simple things you can remember to do when you meet someone who uses a wheelchair.

- When you talk to a person in a wheelchair, talk to them – ignore the wheelchair. The fact that they use a wheelchair has little to do with the way they are.
- Bend or crouch down so that you are on the same level as the person you are speaking to. This will mean that the wheelchair user does not have to crane their neck to speak to you.
- Ask if they want help. Some people in manual wheelchairs may be glad of a little help, but not all wheelchair users want or need help. Ask first.
- Never assume that a person in a wheelchair has other difficulties besides being unable to walk. Some people who use wheelchairs do have other difficulties, but people who use wheelchairs are all different.

At school

Many wheelchair users go to ordinary schools. This may be their local school or, for practical reasons, it may be one a little further away. The school they go to has to have good **access** for their wheelchair, for example, a stair lift or a lift if their classroom is upstairs. They do lessons alongside their classmates, although they may do an alternative activity when it is time for PE. Many people believe that it is important for all kinds of children with different needs and abilities to go to the same schools. They think that this helps us to grow up understanding each other, and each other's needs and different ways of life.

Sometimes ordinary schools cannot meet a young wheelchair user's needs. This may be because they have difficulties other than being unable to walk. For example, they may not have the use of their hands. They may need to use equipment such as specially adapted computers. These children may go to a school with teachers who are specially trained to support them, and with equipment that can help them make the best of their abilities.

Wheelchair users take part in most school activities, including dance shows and theatre performances.

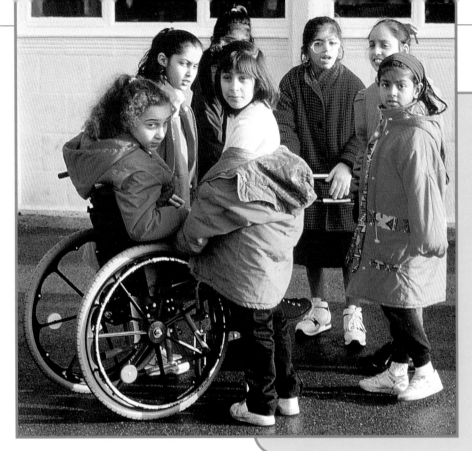

Look around your playground. We are all different in some way. It would be a very boring world if we were all the same. Most of us appreciate the things that are different about our friends, as well as the things we have in common.

Other people

If you are a wheelchair user in an ordinary school, most people will not make an issue of it, but it can make you a target for bullies. Bullies are people who hurt others by calling them names, or by hitting them or pushing them around. Some people pick on others simply because they are different in some way. It may be the clothes they wear, the fact that they wear glasses or that they use a wheelchair.

It can be difficult to know what to do about bullying. Some people find that if they ignore the bully, he or she gets bored and leaves them alone. This is not always the case. You may need to talk to an adult you can trust. They should be able to help the bully to stop behaving in this way. Sometimes it can help if a parent or helper, such as an **occupational therapist**, talks to a class about why someone uses a wheelchair and gives them a chance to ask any questions they have.

At home

What do you do at home? Perhaps you divide your time between homework and chores such as washing up or cleaning your room, and doing the things you really enjoy. Well, that is what children who use wheelchairs do, too! The only difference is that they will be doing some or all of these things from a wheelchair, so their family will have made some alterations around the house to make life easier for them.

Almost all everyday objects can be adapted so that a person in a wheelchair can use them. In the kitchen, it may mean having lower kitchen units so that you can reach to help chop vegetables or wash up. In the bedroom, it may mean having a desk wide and high enough for your wheelchair so you can sit there to do your homework. It helps if spaces between pieces of furniture are wide enough for the wheelchair to pass through easily. Some people may need a bath lift to help them in and out of the bath. Some may use a claw reacher – a special gripper on a long stick – to help them pick things up. Other tricks or gadgets can help, too, such as spring laces, which many children wear today. They are curled into coils that hold your shoes on when you pull them without having to be laced up.

Everyone has jobs to do around the house – and wheelchair users are no exception!

Have a go! – sports and wheelchairs

Doing different sports activities can be good fun and a great way to make friends – with the added bonus that exercise keeps you fit at the same time! Wheelchair users take part in many different sports. You need specially adapted wheelchairs for some sports. For example, racing wheelchairs are very light, and the wheels are angled slightly to make them more stable at high speeds. If you use a wheelchair and you want to have a go at skiing, you can hire a sit-ski, which you sit on, or you can use a sledge, which you can steer. Many artificial ski slopes run training sessions for skiers who use wheelchairs for some or all of the time. For other sports, such as table tennis, people can use their ordinary wheelchairs.

You can also enter many sporting competitions in your wheelchair. There are many tournaments for wheelchair users in a whole range of sports, including basketball, tennis and sailing.

If you use a wheelchair, you may be able to have a go at a variety of different sports at a nearby sports centre. Why not have a go – you never know what hidden sporting talents you might have!

Meet Lee

Hello. My name is Lee and I'm thirteen years old. I have got two sisters and one brother. Kathy is sixteen, Louise is fifteen and my little brother Luke is just a toddler. Luke is gorgeous. I'd do anything for him, he's so cute. I teach him tricks – I just taught him how to blow raspberries and I'm teaching him to crawl. I reckon the first word he says will be 'Lee'!

We've also got a pet. He's a golden retriever called Benji and he's about ten months old. He's a bit of a pain – he pulls the washing off the line and he chews everything. He play fights with me. I lie on the floor, and he jumps on me and licks me. Today, my dad, John, took me to the shops to buy some new toys for Benji. I got him a bone, a big ball and a frisbee. I'm going to try to train him to catch the frisbee.

Mostly I play with the computer or my Play Station when I'm at home. I like fighting games. I like playing Monopoly, too. I play that at school with my friend Neill. I read stories with my mum at home.

I use a wheelchair because I was involved in a car accident when I was four. I'm **paralysed** down one side so I can use one leg and one arm. At school I use a trike. You cycle it like a normal bike. If you cycle with one leg the other leg goes with it and the pedals go round.

At home I can sort of walk using the furniture. I hold onto the walls and sofas and get myself around like that. I can get in and out of bed and things like that all right myself. When we go out I use a wheelchair and my mum or my big sisters usually push me. They take me into town and things. Sometimes people stare at me when I'm out and that's really annoying. If you say something back you only make it worse. I usually just laugh and ignore them. They should really understand that people in wheelchairs are just like them, but we just need a bit more help to do some things.

Glossary

access a place or vehicle with wheelchair access is one that is designed in such a way that wheelchair users can get in and out of it easily

brain control centre of the body. It controls the rest of the body, and how we think, learn, move and feel.

cerebral palsy condition people are born with in which the part of the brain that controls movement has been damaged

condition physical complaint that is not a disease or an illness. A condition is caused by damage to a part of the body and is usually a long term problem.

mobility ability to move around

muscular dystrophy disease that weakens the muscles in a person's body

nerves we have nerves all over our body. They take messages from the body to the brain and back again

occupational therapist someone who is trained to help people with physical difficulties, such as wheelchair users, to live as independently as possible

Paralympics Olympic Games for disabled competitors, held after the summer Olympics. Paralympics include a range of sports including wheelchair racing.

paralysis when you have paralysis in a part of your body, it means that you cannot move it at all

physiotherapist someone who is trained to help others with physical disabilities. For example, they show people how to do exercises to help them move damaged muscles more easily.

speech and language therapist person who advises and helps people who have problems with speaking and listening

spina bifida medical condition people are born with which affects the spine. Because the spinal cord is damaged, some children with spina bifida cannot walk.

spinal cord large nerve that links the brain to the nerves in all the other parts of the body. The spinal cord is protected by the backbone, or spine.

wheelchair service group of people responsible for providing wheelchairs to people who need them

Helpful books and addresses

BOOKS

Body Systems: Moving, Jackie Hardie &
Angela Royston, Heinemann Library,
1997.
*Body Matters: Why Do Bones Break, And
Other Questions About Movement*, Angela
Royston, Heinemann Library, 2002.
I Have Cerebral Palsy, Brenda Pettenuzzo,
Franklin Watts, 1988
Living With Cerebral Palsy, Jenny Bryan,
Wayland, 1998

ORGANIZATIONS AND WEBSITES

The Association of Wheelchair Children
provides support, wheelchair use training
and advice for young wheelchair users.
Their website also has a chatroom.
Head Office
6 Woodman Parade
Woodman Street
North Woolwich
London E16 2ll
Telephone: 0870 121 0050
Website: www.wheelchairchildren.org.uk

Treloar Trust
Provides education, therapy, independence
training and opportunities for young people
(aged 5–25) with physical difficulties, some
of whom also have sensory, communication
or learning difficulties.
Upper Froyle
Alton
Hampshire GU34 4JX
Telephone: 01420 526 526
Fax: 01420 23 957
Website: www.treloar.org.uk

IN AUSTRALIA

NSW Wheelchair Sports Association
PO Box 3160
Putney
NSW 2112
Telephone: 02 98095260
Fax: 02 9809 5638
Website: www.nswwsa.org.au

Wheelchair Sports Association of SA
PO Box 144
Greenacres
SA 5086
Telephone: 08 8349 6366
Fax: 08 8349 6223
Website: www.wheelchairsports-sa.org.au

Australian Wheelchair Athletes
PO Box 4
Mitchell
ACT 2911
Telephone: 02 6242 7720
Fax: 02 6242 7720
Website: www.pcug.org.au

Index

Titles in the *What does it mean to be/have* series include:

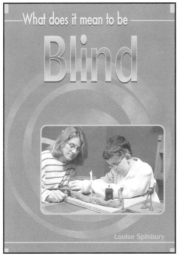

Hardback   0 431 13938 5

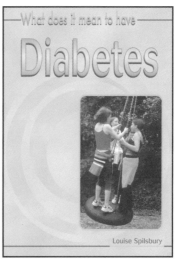

Hardback   0 431 13937 7

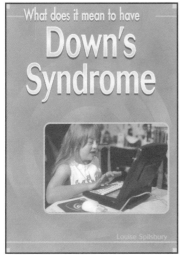

Hardback   0 431 13935 0

Hardback   0 431 13936 9

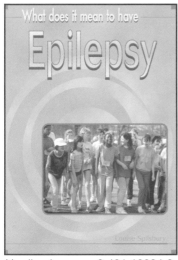

Hardback   0 431 13934 2

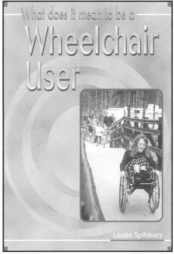

Hardback   0 431 13939 3

Find out about the other titles in this series on our website www.heinemann.co.uk/library